38.00

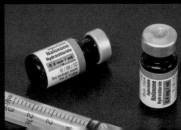

OPIOID EDUCATION

FENTANYL
THE WORLD'S DEADLIEST DRUG

AMY STERLING CASIL

MASON CREST
PHILADELPHIA | MIAMI

MASON CREST

450 Parkway Drive, Suite D, Broomall, Pennsylvania 19008
(866) MCP-BOOK (toll-free) • www.masoncrest.com

Printed and bound in the United States of America.

CPSIA Compliance Information: Batch #OE2019.
For further information, contact Mason Crest at 1-866-MCP-Book.

First printing

ISBN (hardback) 978-1-4222-4379-4
ISBN (series) 978-1-4222-4378-7
ISBN (ebook) 978-1-4222-7426-2

Library of Congress Cataloging-in-Publication Data on file at the Library of Congress

Interior and cover design: Torque Advertising + Design
Interior layout: Tara Raymo, CreativelyTara
Production: Michelle Luke

Publisher's Note: Websites listed in this book were active at the time of publication. The publisher is not responsible for websites that have changed their address or discontinued operation since the date of publication. The publisher reviews and updates the websites each time the book is reprinted.

QR CODES AND LINKS TO THIRD-PARTY CONTENT

CONTENTS

KEY ICONS TO LOOK FOR:

 Words to Understand: These words with their easy-to-understand definitions will increase the reader's understanding of the text while building vocabulary skills.

 Sidebars: This boxed material within the main text allows readers to build knowledge, gain insights, explore possibilities, and broaden their perspectives by weaving together additional information to provide realistic and holistic perspectives.

 Educational videos: Readers can view videos by scanning our QR codes, providing them with additional educational content to supplement the text. Examples include news coverage, moments in history, speeches, iconic sports moments, and much more!

 Text-Dependent Questions: These questions send the reader back to the text for more careful attention to the evidence presented there.

 Research Projects: Readers are pointed toward areas of further inquiry connected to each chapter. Suggestions are provided for projects that encourage deeper research and analysis.

 Series Glossary of Key Terms: This back-of-the-book glossary contains terminology used throughout this series. Words found here increase the reader's ability to read and comprehend higher-level books and articles in this field.

A bag of counterfeit opioid painkiller pills, seized in a Drug Enforcement Agency (DEA) raid, which were found to contain the powerful drug fentanyl. Over the past several years this potent drug has been responsible for tens of thousands of overdose deaths.

WORDS TO UNDERSTAND

autopsy—a medical examination conducted after a person dies to determine the cause of death.

black market—an "underground" or shadow economy dealing in illegal or secret goods such as drugs.

chronic—a long-lasting illness or disease that lasts a long time.

counterfeit—an copy of an authentic original product with the intent to cheat or defraud.

synthetic drugs—drugs created in labs from chemicals, also known as "designer drugs."

CHAPTER 1

WHO USES FENTANYL?

On October 2, 2018, Livermore California police issued a warning to parents about deadly drugs tainted or mixed with fentanyl. The warning came a day after the death of two teens from fentanyl-related overdoses. One of the teens was Justin Miles, the eighteen-year-old stepson of "Dilbert" cartoonist Scott Adams.

Adams immediately made a live video talking about his sorrow in losing Justin and how dangerous fentanyl was. Before Justin died, Adams hadn't even heard of the drug.

Justin's family learned he had become addicted to **counterfeit** Xanax pills provided by a street dealer, and also had a fentanyl patch on his arm at the time of his death.

"Fentanyl probably killed half of the 72,000 Americans who died of drug overdoses in 2017," Adams said. Justin Miles was just one of more than 30,000 people to die of a fentanyl-related overdose since June, 2017—double the number which died from the drug in 2016.

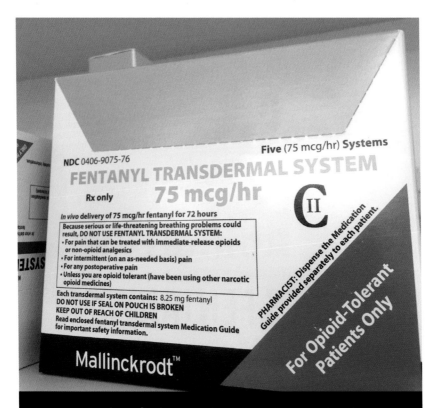

NDC 0406-9075-76

FENTANYL TRANSDERMAL SYSTEM

Rx only   **75 mcg/hr**

Five (75 mcg/hr) **Systems**

C II

In vivo delivery of 75 mcg/hr fentanyl for 72 hours

Because serious or life-threatening breathing problems could
result, DO NOT USE FENTANYL TRANSDERMAL SYSTEM:
• For pain that can be treated with immediate-release opioids
  or non-opioid analgesics
• For intermittent (on an as-needed basis) pain
• For any postoperative pain
• Unless you are opioid tolerant (have been using other narcotic
  opioid medicines)

Each transdermal system contains: 8.25 mg fentanyl
DO NOT USE IF SEAL ON POUCH IS BROKEN
KEEP OUT OF REACH OF CHILDREN
Read enclosed fentanyl transdermal system Medication Guide
for important safety information.

PHARMACIST: Dispense the Medication
Guide provided separately to each patient.

For Opioid-Tolerant
Patients Only

Mallinckrodt™

Fentanyl is classified as a Schedule II drug under the Controlled Substance Act of 1970. This means that the federal government recognizes that it has legitimate medical uses, but that it also has a high potential for abuse. Doctors typically prescribe fentanyl to treat patients with severe pain or to manage pain after surgery.

Fentanyl deaths have doubled every year between 2013 and 2016. The Centers for Disease Control have declared fentanyl "the deadliest drug." Scott Adams said that fentanyl was a tragedy on the level of the Vietnam War. The Vietnam War lasted more than nineteen years and took the lives of more than 59,000 American soldiers. Fentanyl is taking lives much faster.

How Is Fentanyl Legally Used?

Physicians prescribe fentanyl legally to help control pain after surgery. They may also prescribe fentanyl for people who are in extreme pain at the end of their lives, especially cancer patients. Mayo Clinic pain management specialist Dr. Michael Hooten said that fentanyl is more dangerous than other opiates because it is "many, many times more potent than morphine, oxycodone, Oxycontin, Vicodin, Dilaudid, hydromorphone" and other similar pain medications.

Cancer patients or others with persistent pain can experience "breakthrough" pain. Breakthrough pain means severe pain that "breaks through" less potent pain medication. Fentanyl can help to relieve breakthrough pain. Fentanyl is also legally used as anesthesia for patients who are having open heart surgery. It may also be used during other types of surgery on people whose hearts aren't functioning well.

Fentanyl is also prescribed for people who have taken other kinds of pain medication and developed a tolerance.

RELIEVING CHRONIC PAIN

Fibromyalgia is a medical condition that causes pain in skin, muscles and joints. "Rainydaygirl" has fibromyalgia and is one of 622 patients who reported using fentanyl patches to relieve chronic pain on a patient user website. She used a fentanyl patch with a 25 mcg (microgram) dose for more than 14 years safely to relieve chronic pain.

Legendary rocker Tom Petty was using fentanyl to manage the chronic pain caused by a hip injury while on tour during 2017. He died of an accidental overdose.

In 2017, legendary guitarist Tom Petty performed more than fifty shows in severe pain due to a partial hip fracture. Physicians prescribed a fentanyl patch to help with his severe pain. After Petty's family found him collapsed in his music studio, he was rushed to the hospital where he died from an accidental overdose. Petty's **autopsy** found that the rock star had supplemented the painkilling properties of the prescribed patch by ingesting other forms of fentanyl which were not legal.

Patches are the most common way medical fentanyl is used. Other forms of legally prescribed fentanyl include lozenges, oral swabs, nasal sprays, and injections. Fentanyl in pill form is not prescribed or legal.

How Is Fentanyl Illegally Used?

Many people use illegal fentanyl without realizing it. Some dealers sell pills that they advertise as common pain medication like Percocet or OxyContin. In reality, these counterfeit pills often have fentanyl as an ingredient.

Pain patients can turn to dealers because they develop a tolerance to ordinary pain medication. In narcotics or opioid tolerance, people need to take more and more of the medication to feel the same effect. Addiction psychiatrist Scott Bienenfeld says, "the majority of my patients are pain patients and someone gave them fentanyl as an add-on: 'You've taken OxyContin, now take this.'"

Drug dealers don't tell their customers that the "add-on" is really fentanyl. Illegal opioid pills containing fentanyl showed up on the **black market** starting in 2007, when doctors started to write fewer prescriptions of legal opiates like OxyContin.

The practice of "cutting" illegal drugs that are sold as powder, then injected by drug users, started years ago when street drug dealers mixed inexpensive and harmless substances like powdered sugar, corn starch, powdered milk, or baby formula into heroin or cocaine. One of the deadliest changes to occur in recent years is the dealer switch from making their drugs weaker to making them stronger by adding fentanyl.

What is the motive for dealers to mix fentanyl with heroin and cocaine? Even if they don't tell customers, the mixture causes stronger, faster, and more addictive "highs." Although fatal overdoses can occur in as little as a minute, dealers are willing to take the chance that instead of killing their customers, they will make them even more addicted.

A drug-cutting table, used for processing fentanyl. Because fentanyl is inexpensive to make, it is often added to drugs like heroin and cocaine to increase their potency and make the illegal drugs more profitable for the dealers.

To see a young fentanyl addict tell her story, scan here:

Who are the Users Who get Fentanyl Unintentionally?

Counterfeit opioid pills are not only sold by street dealers. Some are sold online and shipped to the US and other countries. The pills are made in China and have fentanyl mixed with other opiates. The most dangerous type contain **synthetic**, lab-created concentrated fentanyl which can be 50 to 100 times stronger than legal, medically prescribed fentanyl.

The majority of musicians who died from fentanyl overdoses probably didn't know they were taking fentanyl. They thought they were taking a medication they had taken before, like OxyContin. When Prince was found dead at his

Rapper Lil Peep was only twenty-one when he took counterfeit pills he thought were the anti-anxiety drug Xanax in November 2017. Instead, the pills contained fentanyl, and he died of an unintentional overdose.

Paisley Park home in 2016, investigators found 49 black market pills which were partially made of fentanyl. Prince's friends and family told investigators that he thought he was taking Vicodin, a common pain medication provided for tooth aches and muscle pains. After a two year investigation turned up no suspects, it's unlikely that the dealer or friend who gave the pills to Prince will ever be caught or punished.

Which Regions are Most Affected by Fentanyl?

The Centers for Disease Control's (CDC) Midwest region includes Illinois, Indiana, Iowa, Kansas, Michigan, Minnesota, Missouri, Nebraska, North Dakota, Ohio, South Dakota and

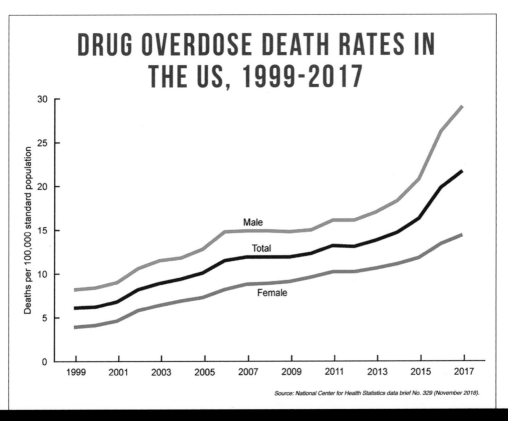

DRUG OVERDOSE DEATH RATES IN THE US, 1999-2017

Deaths per 100,000 standard population

Male

Total

Female

Source: National Center for Health Statistics data brief No. 329 (November 2018).

The rate of drug overdose deaths increased from 6.1 per 100,000 people in 1999 to 21.7 in 2017. The rate rose by 10 percent a year from 1999 through 2006, by 3 percent a year from 2006 through 2014, and by 16 percent a year from 2014 through 2017. Throughout this period, overdose rates were significantly higher for males (rising from 8.2 per 100,000 population in 1999 to 29.1 in 2017) than females (an increase from 3.9 in 1999 to 14.4 in 2017).

Wisconsin. Emergency departments in these states saw a 70 percent increase in overdoses between July 2016 and September 2017.

The CDC reported more than 70,000 deaths due to drug overdose between May 2017 and May 2018, more than auto crashes, HIV/AIDS, or gun violence killed in their highest total years. Fentanyl and a few other less-common synthetic opioids were the largest and fastest-growing category of overdose causes, leading to more than 30,000 deaths.

New England states including Vermont, New Hampshire, and Massachusetts, experienced the opioid epidemic and onslaught of fentanyl earlier than other states. Their law enforcement and health officials launched anti-opioid education and overdose prevention programs. These states saw declines in fentanyl overdose deaths between 2016 and 2017.

US Midwest and Mid-Atlantic states saw major increases in fentanyl and other opioid deaths between 2017 and 2018. In New Jersey, opioid overdose deaths rose by 27 percent, while Ohio, Indiana, and West Virginia saw overdose death rate increases of more than 17 percent. Powdered brown or white heroin, much of which is sold as Asian heroin, is the common type of heroin sold in these states. Dealers easily mix fentanyl into powdered heroin and may or may not inform customers it is present in their products.

Western states may have lower rates of overdose death than Midwest or Mid-Atlantic states because "black tar" heroin is more commonly sold in these areas, brought in from Mexico. Because it is black or dark brown and sticky, black tar heroin is much harder for dealers to mix with fentanyl powder to produce a more powerful, deadly mix. Dr. Chris Jones, head of the national mental health and substance abuse laboratory, told the New York Times that dealers were finding ways to mix fentanyl into black tar heroin, so overdoses could soon increase in western US states.

Cities in Crisis

Fatal heroin deaths began to decline in Maryland in 2016, but deaths due to fentanyl continued to increase. The city of Baltimore had by far the most deaths in the state in 2017, with

Fentanyl overdoses are such a problem in Baltimore that federal and state authorities have launched an effort to educate the public about the danger of the drug through billboards and community meetings. City police have been instructed to crack down on illegal fentanyl labs and distribution networks.

DRUG OVERDOSE DEATHS, BY US STATE, 2017

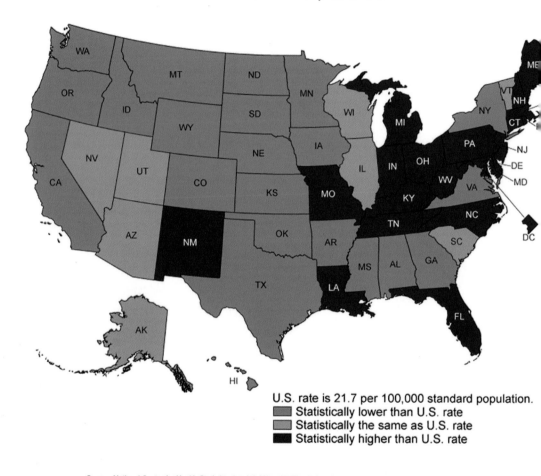

U.S. rate is 21.7 per 100,000 standard population.
- Statistically lower than U.S. rate
- Statistically the same as U.S. rate
- Statistically higher than U.S. rate

Source: National Center for Health Statistics data brief No. 329 (November 2018).

In 2017, twenty states and the District of Columbia had drug overdose death rates that were higher than the national average of 21.7 deaths per 100,000 population. West Virginia (57.8), Ohio (46.3), and Pennsylvania (44.3) were the three states with the highest drug overdose death rates, followed by the District of Columbia (44.0).

The numbers continued to climb in 2018, with more than 2,000 fentanyl-related deaths throughout the state, 88 percent of which were due to fentanyl overdoses.

In January 2017, Dayton, Ohio, was considered an epicenter of fentanyl overdoses and deaths and was even named the "overdose capital of America." The city experienced eighty-one drug overdoses in May 2017 alone. Out of a population of about 140,000, Dayton officials realized that if the trend continued, more than 1,000 local residents might lose their lives to opioid overdoses before the end of the year. Desperate to stop the epidemic, the city established a new emergency response program with education, hospitals, law enforcement, and community organizations. By June of 2018, opioid-related emergency room visits and overdose deaths in Dayton had declined by 60 percent.

Louisville, Kentucky, experienced forty-three overdoses on a single day in 2017. None of these cities topped Chicago, Illinois, for overdoses that didn't result in death. In 2017, Chicago's hospitals reported seventy-four overdoses in a single seventy-two hour period.

Although large cities often receive a lot of negative publicity when fentanyl deaths are reported by urban hospitals and emergency responders, smaller communities and rural areas are also affected by fentanyl. CDC researcher Rita Noonan, who grew up in a rural community, wrote that accidental death rates from auto crashes, falls, and drug overdoses are about 50 percent higher in rural areas than cities. Between 1999 and 2015, death rates from opioids have quadrupled for young people between 18 and 25. Among rural women of any age, overdose death rates have tripled.

Fifty-nine people in Chicago died from fentanyl overdoses in 2017. These numbers don't tell the whole story. Drugs spread fast on Chicago's "Heroin Highway." A Chicago drug reduction organization gave out more than 10,000 vials of overdose drug naloxone (Narcan) in 2015, and users reported more than 5,700 were successfully used.

How does Narcan keep the Epidemic Going?

A drug known as Narcan reverses the effects of opioids on breathing and the nervous system that cause an overdose and can lead to death. It comes in three forms: injectable, a self-injecting pen like an EpiPen for allergic reactions, and a nasal spray. Narcan is available without a prescription in pharmacies in forty-six states. Many first responders, such as police and paramedics, carry multiple doses of Narcan and its use has increased dramatically over the past five years. Some drug dealers even provide Narcan to their regular customers.

Before Narcan became widely used, if several people overdosed on heroin in a city or neighborhood, word would get out about the bad batch of drugs. Today, some drug addicts feel "safe" if they have Narcan, which makes them more willing to try stronger drugs. A drug user named David Harek told Fusion Magazine that he had started using heroin and fentanyl as a teen. By the time he was twenty-seven, he had overdosed six times, using Narcan each time to reverse the overdose and save his life. If heroin addicts know that someone else overdosed on heroin or fentanyl, David said that others will want to try the drug for themselves. "It must be good," he said. "You're gonna do exactly what they did. It's just the name of the addiction."

Who Is Most At-Risk for a Fentanyl Overdose?

Middle-aged and older adults are among those with the highest risk. Terminally ill cancer patients and others with **chronic** illnesses who are in severe pain are prescribed fentanyl. Many others purchase pain pills that they think are prescriptions they have taken before, only to receive a black-market pill made with potentially deadly fentanyl. According to the Centers for Disease Control, about half of the people who died from opioid overdoses in 2013 and 2014 were ages 45 to 64.

Older people may be injured or have other conditions leading to chronic pain. They start taking prescribed opioids like Vicodin or OxyContin. Opioid users develop tolerance to the medication which loses its effectiveness over time. Seeking more relief, older pain patients switch to stronger medications, often combining them with other medications. Fentanyl is so strong that when added to other medications or alcohol, it can easily cause an overdose.

Young adults between the ages of eighteen and twenty-four are also at risk. Young people who have used prescription drugs (often found in home medicine cabinets) can "graduate" to using street drugs like heroin and cocaine. Opiate tolerance means that larger amounts of the drug are needed to produce a high. Fentanyl is so powerful that the intense high combined with the knowledge that Narcan is available to reverse overdoses represents an almost irresistible desire to keep using the drug.

Some young users, knowing how strong fentanyl is, will heat their parents' cancer pain relief patches to mix the gel with street heroin and inject it. Even a single grain of synthetic concentrated fentanyl could be deadly. Powdered heroin and cocaine sold on the streets may be mixed with this type of mega-fentanyl, leading to overdose risk.

About 80 percent of people who use heroin started out misusing prescription pain medication that a physician may have provided for injuries. Young adults are at the greatest risk of this type of opioid misuse. Fentanyl is so powerful that even a single use may result in addiction.

TEXT-DEPENDENT QUESTIONS

1. Why are older adults (ages 45-64) at the highest risk of fentanyl overdose?
2. How could naloxone (Narcan), the antidote for opioid overdoses, contribute to fentanyl deaths over time?
3. Why was Dayton, Ohio, called the "overdose capital of America?"

RESEARCH PROJECT

Have you heard of fentanyl-related overdoses in your community? For this research project, consult your local media (newspaper websites, radio or television), local substance use counseling, hospitals, or treatment organizations, and local government websites. You may also interview law enforcement officers, school counselors, or teachers with expert knowledge. Also speak to family members and friends about opioid use, fentanyl, and overdoses. Discover how many people have been affected in your community. When you have completed your interviews, analyze the information you have learned. Compare your community to some of the cities or rural areas mentioned in the chapter. Write a one-page essay communicating your comparisons and analysis to your peers. List the sources you used at the end of your essay.

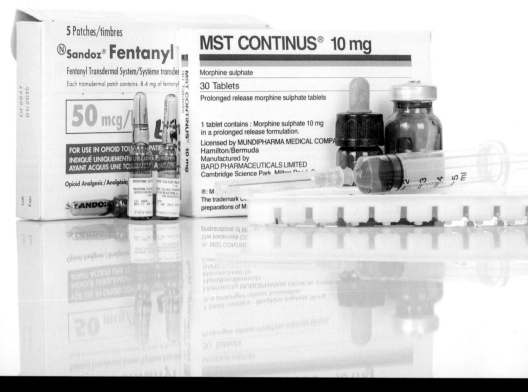

Fentanyl was created in the 1960s to replace another drug, morphine, that was used to reduce pain in patients with cancer and other health problems. Both drugs are opioids, but fentanyl is considerably more potent—its effect is roughly 100 times stronger than morphine.

WORDS TO UNDERSTAND

fat-soluble—a chemical compound that can dissolve in fats and oils, including the body's own fat cells.

illicit—something that is forbidden by law, customs, or rules.

patent—a legal term for the exclusive right to make, use, and sell an invention, which can include medicines. Patents are issued by the patent offices in different countries for specific periods of time.

CHAPTER 2

THE HISTORY OF FENTANYL

Fentanyl was invented in 1960 after years of research by one of the most renowned pharmaceutical chemists of all time, Dr. Paul Janssen. For several years, the Belgian scientist had been working to create new synthetic medications to relieve pain. In 1957, Dr. Janssen's team synthesized phenoperidine (Operidine) which is similar to morphine and is used for anesthesia. Then, the team synthesized fentanyl: 100 times stronger than morphine and the strongest opioid in the world when it was created.

The Creation of Fentanyl

The man who created fentanyl is famous among biomedical researchers. Dr. Paul Janssen was born in Belgium in 1926. He founded one of the world's largest pharmaceutical companies,

When Paul Janssen was in high school, his four-year-old sister came down with meningitis, a bacterial infection that causes swelling of the brain. At the time, there were no antibiotics to treat the disease, and his sister died. He vowed to devote his life to medical research to invent new medicines that would save lives and reduce pain and suffering.

Janssen Pharmaceutica, with more than 40,000 employees today. Known to friends and colleagues as "Dr. Paul," he often asked chemists in his labs, "What's new?" Janssen is credited with discovering more than eighty new active chemical compounds with medical benefits, including five that are on the World Health Organization's list of essential medicines. Fentanyl is one of the five "essential medicines."

At the time his lab synthesized fentanyl, the team's goal was to create a new fast-acting, strong opioid to be used as an anesthetic that wouldn't cause nausea or affect heart function during surgery. Janssen's team also realized that morphine and similar natural opiates took time to take effect because they could not easily penetrate into the nervous system. He focused on making **fat-soluble** opiate molecules with a chemical structure that could bind to pain receptors in the brain, the team ended up creating fentanyl.

Combined with fentanyl's ability to quickly relieve severe pain, the medication was adopted throughout Western

European countries in the early 1960s. Fentanyl would have to wait until 1968 before it was approved by the US Food and Drug Administration (FDA) due to early concerns over its strength and potential for abuse.

How Was Fentanyl Used for Pain Relief?

Janssen Pharmaceutica developed fentanyl as a surgical anesthetic and as a potential pain reliever. In the 1960s, doctors in Western Europe used fentanyl as an intravenous pain reliever in hospitals.

Fentanyl's chemical structure meant that in some forms like nasal sprays, pain relief could occur within seconds. Other forms, like transdermal (skin) patches or lollipops, could spread smaller doses of pain-relieving fentanyl out over

The European drug company Janssen Pharmaceutica originally developed and marketed fentanyl during the 1960s. Today, the company is part of the major American corporation Johnson & Johnson.

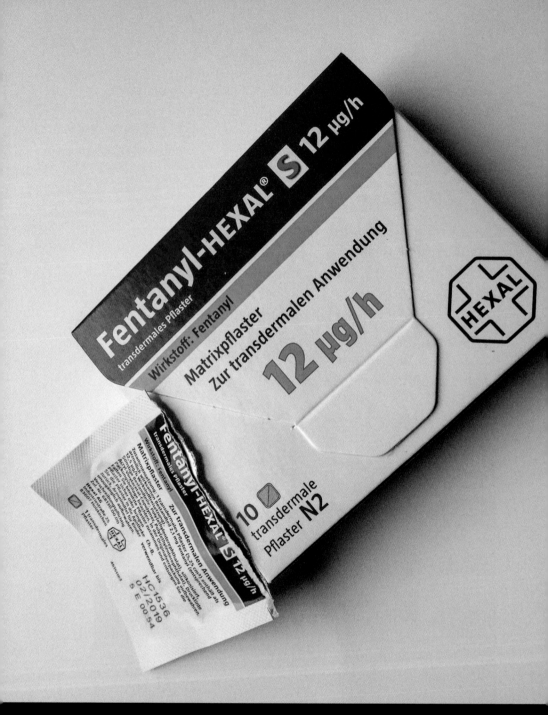

Fentanyl transdermal patches were prescribed in many countries to manage severe chronic pain. This package of fentanyl patches was sold in Germany.

longer periods of time. Up until the 1980s, fentanyl was used primarily for surgical anesthesia, not pain relief.

The original **patent** for fentanyl expired in 1981. This meant that other companies could develop new ways to deliver fentanyl without paying the patent holder (Dr. Janssen's company and later, Johnson & Johnson). In the 1980s, a company in California called Alza developed a transdermal fentanyl patch for chronic pain patients, especially people with cancer. The patch, marketed under the name of Duragesic, provided pain relief spread out over two to three days. Duragesic ended up being one of the most successful pain relieving products in history. In 2004, the last year the pain-relieving patch was under patent, Alza recorded sales of $2.4 billion in Duragesic patches.

Illegal Uses and Overdoses

Fentanyl wasn't approved for use in the United States for eight years after its invention because FDA officials and prominent physicians like Dr. Robert Phipps from the University of Pennsylvania believed it was too strong and had too much potential for abuse. Fentanyl was created in a lab, and its chemical structure could be duplicated in a lab—legal or not.

Illegal uses of fentanyl emerged in the 1970s, initially among medical professionals who had access to the prescription drug. In the late 1970s, illegal fentanyl was sold in California as "China White." (This name has been used to refer to many different narcotics, including heroin, heroin and fentanyl mixtures, and pure fentanyl.) Fentanyl's first known victims were two California men who died of overdoses in 1979. Over the next year, 100 people in California died from injecting the white powder they thought was heroin, but which was really fentanyl.

Another fentanyl-abuse situation took the lives of eighteen people in Philadelphia during 1988. The overdose outbreaks involved smaller amounts of illegal fentanyl and local distribution. Authorities were able to stop the outbreaks by tracing the drugs to local illegal labs and shutting them down.

Off-Label Prescriptions Increase

If a doctor prescribes a regulated medicine like fentanyl for a non-officially approved use, it is called an "off-label" prescription. In 2005, the Food and Drug Administration (FDA) started to investigate misuse of Duragesic fentanyl patches—the investigation resulted in a 2007 warning to doctors and patients about potential misuse. Some patients overdosed from combining patches with other opiates. **Illicit** drug users wore the patches and took other opiates, and also began to heat the patches to collect fentanyl-rich gel for injection.

Actiq is a fentanyl lollipop that was developed in the 1990s. The lollipop's sweet taste and effectiveness made it popular with many pain patients. By 2006, a study by ImpactRx found that up to 80 percent of Actiq lollipops were prescribed for patients who weren't officially authorized to have the drug. Actiq lollipops are made with sugar and patients can use them "as needed" for pain. As a result, many people who used Actiq suffered tooth decay, including one patient who eventually lost all of his teeth.

Actiq was and is popular on the streets. Lollipops stolen from pharmacies or obtained through prescription fraud are sold as "perc-a-pops" (referring to the opioid Percocet) or "morphine lollipops," although they're made from fentanyl, not morphine. The lollipops have just as much potential for overdose whether they are legally or illegally obtained.

The amount of misuse of legally manufactured fentanyl,

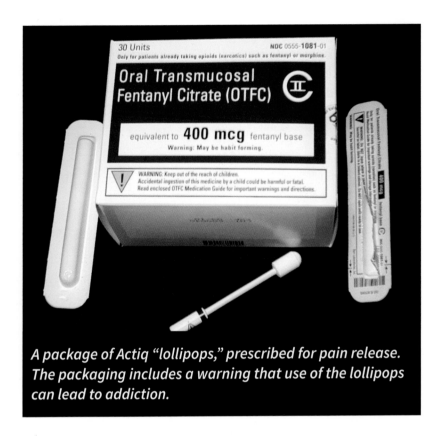

A package of Actiq "lollipops," prescribed for pain release. The packaging includes a warning that use of the lollipops can lead to addiction.

whether in patch or lollipop form, has stayed relatively steady since the 2000s. Most of the growth in fentanyl misuse and deadly overdoses has come from illegal fentanyl, whether mixed with heroin or other street drugs, or pressed into counterfeit pills that deceive the user into thinking they are common prescription opiates like Vicodin or Percocet.

Massive Amounts of Illicitly Manufactured Fentanyl Arrive

Law enforcement and health officials refer to illegally made fentanyl as Illicitly Manufactured Fentanyl, or IMF. Throughout the 2000s, IMF was made by smaller labs in the US and Mexico.

To see how fentanyl has contributed to the opioid crisis, scan here:

2015

Vox analysis | German Lopez

—52,000 deaths—

Gun violence   Car crash   Drug overdose

Most IMF is made in other countries, especially China. In 2007, US drug enforcement agents raided and closed an illicit fentanyl lab in Mexico which stemmed the tide for a short time.

The amounts that have been imported into the United States began to rise sharply in 2015. IMF can take many forms. According to the CDC, "IMF is often mixed with heroin and/or cocaine or pressed into counterfeit pills—with or without the user's knowledge." The majority of the IMF from China enters the US through Mexico, Canada, and even through the US Mail. It is so easy for IMF to be made in China because the country's pharmaceutical industry is poorly monitored and regulated.

In 2015, DEA officials confiscated 200 pounds of fentanyl—they had seized only eight pounds the year before. In addition to illicit fentanyl from China, illegal labs in the US also can and do make fentanyl. Instructions on how to make fentanyl are available online. Between 2015 and 2016, drug samples submitted for testing by law enforcement agencies to the National Forensic Laboratory Information System (NFLIS), a program of the Drug Enforcement Administration (DEA), that tested positive for fentanyl more than doubled. In 2016, more than 31,700 fentanyl-positive submissions were made to the NFLIS, and they came from local and regional law enforcement agencies across the United States.

Illegal fentanyl and heroin that was seized by the Drug Enforcement Agency (DEA) in a New York City bust in 2018.

In 2016, Thomas Frieden, director of the Centers for Disease Control and Protection, said, "As overdose deaths involving heroin more than quadrupled since 2010, what was a slow stream of illicit fentanyl, a synthetic opioid 50 to 100 times stronger than morphine, is now a flood."

Drug enforcement agents in Canada and the United States have tracked several different ways that illicitly manufactured fentanyl has entered the United States. In 2012, fentanyl-laced heroin was seized in British Columbia and more ended up in Maine in 2013. Counterfeit opiate pills were sold in Montreal, Louisiana, and Rhode Island in 2013. Vancouver has

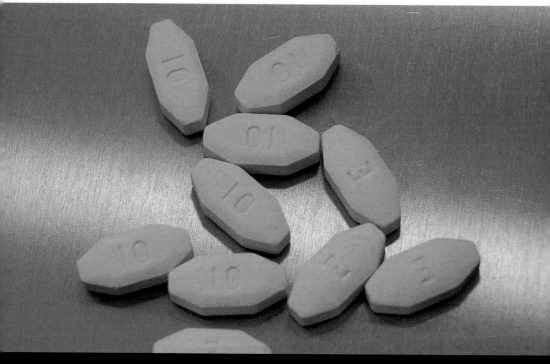

Counterfeit opioid painkillers sold illegally in the United States are often laced with fentanyl. This makes it impossible for users to know exactly what they are taking, making overdoses more common.

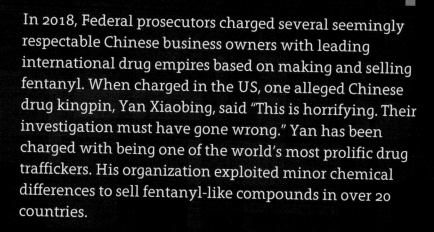

In 2018, Federal prosecutors charged several seemingly respectable Chinese business owners with leading international drug empires based on making and selling fentanyl. When charged in the US, one alleged Chinese drug kingpin, Yan Xiaobing, said "This is horrifying. Their investigation must have gone wrong." Yan has been charged with being one of the world's most prolific drug traffickers. His organization exploited minor chemical differences to sell fentanyl-like compounds in over 20 countries.

a high volume of trade with China in general and has served as a point of entry for IMF to Canada and the United States. Canada doesn't search parcels sent through the mail which weigh less than 30 grams without sufficient cause. Because fentanyl is so powerful, a small package can produce many counterfeit pills or be cut into heroin for high profits.

By the beginning of 2017, reports of IMF came from 30 US states, primarily on the east and west coast of the US and the Canadian border.

A Fentanyl Overdose Epidemic

The Drug Enforcement Administration has documented how cheaply made fentanyl from China is driving the fentanyl death epidemic. $1,000 worth of heroin bought in Mississippi

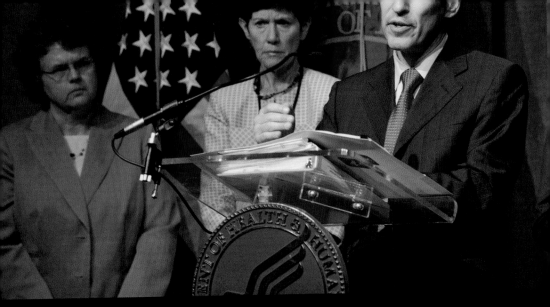

Dr. Thomas Frieden, director of the Centers for Disease Control, has warned about the danger of illegal fentanyl.

could earn a dealer a profit of $4,000. US dealers can buy $1,000 worth of Chinese fentanyl or similar fentanyl-like substances and make a profit of $7.8 million. Only one kilogram of illicitly manufactured fentanyl (IMF) can produce hundreds of thousands of counterfeit prescription pills and tens of millions in profit for drug dealers.

In 2015, US law enforcement seizures of illegal fentanyl increased by more than 426 percent over 2014. According to the Centers for Disease Control, 9,580 people died from fentanyl overdoses in 2015, and by 2016, 19,413 people lost their lives due to fentanyl. In 2017, the death toll was 28,466. Not every fentanyl overdose death is recorded in every state, so the total may be higher.

The current crisis is so severe that drug overdoses have become the top cause of death for US adults under age 55. US life expectancy has declined every year since 2015, in large part due to fentanyl's deadly effects. Fentanyl has struck hardest in West Virginia, which suffered 38 deaths from fentanyl per 100,000 residents in 2017, and New Hampshire, which suffered a rate of 30 deaths per 100,000.

This package of illegal fentanyl, intended for Texas, was intercepted by federal agents in Ohio. To combat the opioid crisis, the federal government has trained hundreds of local law enforcement officers on the "dark net"—areas of the Internet that are hidden from public view, which allow anonymous drug purchases online using "virtual currencies" like Bitcoins.

"If we're talking about counting the bodies, where they lie, and the cause of death, we're talking about a fentanyl crisis," public health scientist John Zibbell told the New York Times in November 2017.

Some health officials think that the epidemic may have reached its peak, with many states experiencing a leveling of overdose deaths in the first half of 2018. Dayton, Ohio was one of the cities hardest hit by fentanyl overdoses but reduced its death rate through a community-wide effort, from 548 deaths in 2017 to fewer than 250 in 2018. In 2015, the state of Ohio increased the availability of free mental health and substance use disorder treatment services, including medication-assisted treatment, which is also credited with reducing fentanyl overdose deaths statewide, including Dayton.

TEXT-DEPENDENT QUESTIONS

1. Actiq fentanyl lollipops for patients with severe pain are made with sugar and have caused some patients to lose all their teeth due to decay. What are some other ways you can think of to make a fentanyl pain-relieving medication that could provide small doses of pain relief over time that wouldn't cause tooth decay?
2. What do you think the inventor of fentanyl, Dr. Paul Janssen, would say if he learned the medicine he created for heart surgeries and pain has become such a deadly overdose drug?
3. Do you think that the benefits of fentanyl for medical use are worth the risk of illicitly manufactured fentanyl (IMF) and many thousands of lives lost to overdoses?

RESEARCH PROJECT

Dr. Paul Janssen was motivated to create new medicines to cure disease because his four-year-old sister died of meningitis when he was in high school. He ended up creating hundreds of medicines and founding a major company that develops and markets medicine. Using websites or your school library, read more about Dr. Paul Janssen. Dr. Janssen developed five different medications including fentanyl that are on the World Health Organization's list of "essential medicines." Choose one of the other four medicines Dr. Paul Janssen developed that are on the World Health Organization's "essential medicines" list. Learn about that medicine, which medical conditions it can help, and how it is used. Write a two paragraph essay that describes the medicine, how it is used, and which medical conditions it helps. Include your sources at the end of the essay.

Fentanyl can come in several forms, including pills and crystals.

 WORDS TO UNDERSTAND

agonist—a substance which produces a biological response when combined with a receptor.

dopamine—a chemical neurotransmitter that transfers information between neurons, the operating cells of the nervous system and brain.

endorphin—a natural hormone the body secretes to relieve pain by binding to opioid receptors.

euphoria—a feeling of extreme happiness and well-being.

neuron—a specialized cell in the brain and other parts of the body that transmits nerve impulses.

receptor—a molecule in the cells of the brain that allow a natural or synthetic chemical substance to bind to the cells.

CHAPTER 3

HOW DOES FENTANYL WORK?

Fentanyl is a synthetic opioid with a chemical structure similar to natural substances that are made by our own brains or which come from natural sources. The milky-white juice from opium poppies has been used to relieve pain or induce sleep since at least the third century BCE. Inside the juice are bioactive compounds called alkaloids. Naturally derived medications from opium poppies include morphine and codeine. Our own brains naturally make endogenous opioid compounds to relieve pain and stress. Whether or not a chemical compound is called an opioid depends upon whether or not it binds to opioid **receptors** in the brain: specialized cells that developed as part of the body's natural defense systems against pain, injury, and stress.

What are Synthetic Opioids?

Ancient Greeks knew that the juice of opium poppies could relieve pain or induce sleep, but they didn't know why. Once scientists uncovered how opiates (medications derived from opium poppies) took effect on the nervous system by binding to opioid receptors, they began to gain the ability to develop partially or completely lab-created chemicals that could have a similar effect.

Synthetic drugs are made in a lab from basic chemical building blocks. Chemists use a variety of tools and chemical reactions to create drugs which have specific chemical properties intended to provide a medical use such as relieving pain by blocking pain receptors.

Two early synthetic opioids were developed in German labs in the 1930s. The first was pethidine (Demerol) and the second was methadone. Both medications continue to have medical uses. Methadone is used to relieve the withdrawal symptoms of heroin addicts without producing a "high."

Morphine, the most common drug made from opium poppies, was crystallized from opium over 200 years ago. Although morphine relieves pain, even the man who discovered it in 1805, Friedrich Sertürner, recognized that it was addictive and had potentially dangerous side effects. Morphine is ten times stronger than opium due to its concentration, but it is still a naturally derived, not synthetic opioid.

When Dr. Paul Janssen's laboratory worked on creating fentanyl, their goal was to combine basic chemical building blocks to produce a more effective pain reliever and anesthetic for use in surgery. They created a drug that was much more fat-soluble than morphine, which resulted in fentanyl's greater strength—up to 100 times stronger than morphine.

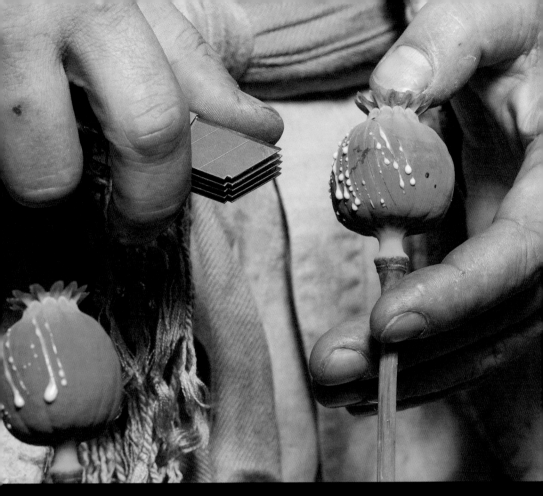

White sap from the opium poppy (papaver somniferum) is collected and processed into opium, a drug that can be further refined into more potent forms like morphine or heroin. Fentanyl is a synthetic drug that mimics the effects of the natural opiates.

The strength of a drug comes from its bioavailability, which means how easily and quickly the body responds to the drug. Fentanyl patches have 92 percent bioavailability, which means nearly all of the drug on a patch will enter the body and bind to opioid receptors in the brain. If fentanyl is injected, 100 percent of it will be used. In contrast, morphine is only 18 to 25 percent bioavailable, depending upon how it is administered.

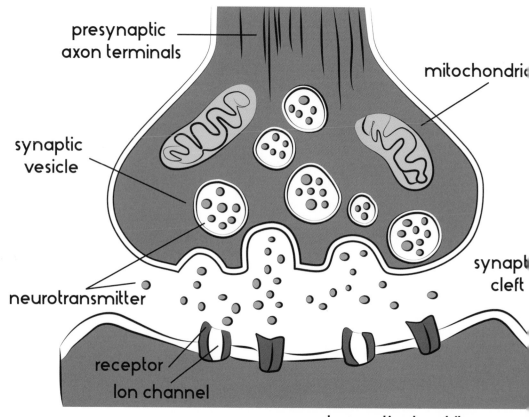

presynaptic
axon terminals

mitochondri[a]

synaptic
vesicle

neurotransmitter

synap[tic]
cleft

receptor

Ion channel

postsynaptic dendrite

Drugs alter the way people think, feel, and behave by disrupting communication between nerve cells (neurons) in the brain. Neurons are separated by small spaces called synapses. Messages are passed from cell to cell across the synapse by specialized molecules, called neurotransmitters, which bind to receptors on the nerve cells. Fentanyl and other opioids produce effects that are similar to—but stronger than—those produced by the neurotransmitters endorphin and enkephalin: reduced pain, decreased alertness, and slowed respiration.

How Does Fentanyl Relieve Pain?

Our body has its own system to relieve pain and stress called the endogenous opioid system. Endogenous means created internally. Within our brains and nervous system, specialized cells called **neurons** can produce natural chemicals called **endorphins** or enkephalins. These chemicals bind to opioid receptors in our brain, spinal cord, or elsewhere in the nervous system. They send a chemical message through opioid receptors that the body isn't in pain. Endorphins also cause the body to release neurochemicals, especially **dopamine**, that relieve stress and anxiety. Other effects include slower breathing and heart rate.

Think about a time you may have fallen while skateboarding. Did you skin a knee or sprain an ankle? You were probably in pain, breathing fast, and your heart was racing. Your body's endorphins kicked in and helped to make the pain less, slowed down your breathing, and helped you feel calmer.

Fentanyl works in the same way. The difference is that it is even faster-acting due to its chemical composition. It also doesn't just help people feel calmer or reduce pain. It produces a very strong "high" or euphoric effect. While natural endorphins slow breathing and heart rate when we're alarmed due to an accident or injury, fentanyl slows these body functions even more. The effects can happen within seconds. These effects are how fentanyl overdoses occur.

How Does Fentanyl Addiction Occur?

Our nervous system has four categories of opioid receptors. Each serves a different purpose in relieving pain, stress, or anxiety. Three receptors are named after Greek letters: mu

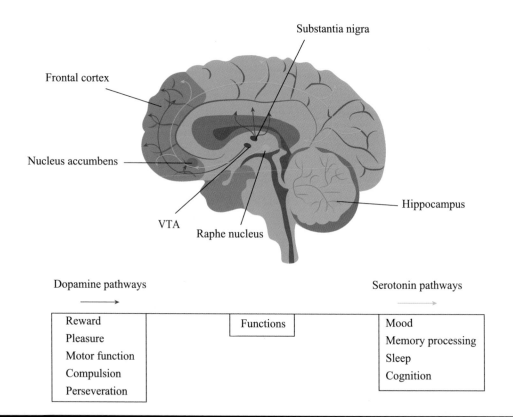

Dopamine pathways

Serotonin pathways

Reward	Functions	Mood
Pleasure		Memory processing
Motor function		Sleep
Compulsion		Cognition
Perseveration		

When fentanyl binds to the body's opioid receptors, the body releases large quantities of the neurotransmitter dopamine to the brain's "reward" areas. This produces a state of euphoria and relaxation.

(MOP), kappa (KOP), and delta (DOP). The fourth receptor is the nocipeptin orphanin receptor or NOP. Natural endorphins made by our bodies have a strong affinity to bind to mu, kappa, and delta receptors, while another body chemical, dynorphin, binds to the NOP receptor.

When a drug binds to one of the opioid receptors, it is called an agonist. Fentanyl is an agonist with a high affinity for the MOP, the mu opioid receptor and a low affinity for the kappa opioid receptor (KOP). It doesn't bind to the other receptors at all.

When fentanyl was first presented for approval in the United States in 1961, a prominent anesthesiologist, Dr. Robert Dripps, opposed its approval because he believed it was too strong and too potentially addictive. Although much of today's understanding of addiction occurred after 1961, Dr. Dripps knew from experience how addictive opioids could be. He reasoned that a drug 100 times stronger than morphine, which was already known to produce addiction and overdoses, must also be highly addictive.

When fentanyl docks on the mu receptor (MOP), the receptor calms the body and relieves anxiety and pain by instructing other parts of the brain to release dopamine. Dopamine is another brain chemical that provides a natural reward and feeling of well-being for doing something that evolution has shown to be beneficial.

Dopamine and Addiction

Dopamine is another brain chemical, similar to endorphins, which provides a "feel good" reward for performing physically beneficial actions. Humans aren't the only living creatures with this chemical; animal brains also produce dopamine. Scientists use the cycle of dopamine rewards and reinforcement to study animal behavior and, by extension, human behavior. For example, if a capuchin monkey presses a lever in its cage and receives a juicy grape as a reward, the monkey's brain will send a happy dopamine signal causing the monkey to eagerly press the level for more grapes. Similarly, lab rats will perform many tasks in a lab to receive rewards of food or water. Dopamine in their brains keeps them coming back for more

Swiss scientist Dr. Christian Lüscher showed how repeated doses of dopamine could permanently change the brain. He attached an optical sensor to the brains of experimental mice which gave them dopamine every time they pressed a lever. After a short time, mice kept pressing the lever, preferring to get dopamine to sleep, water, or food. "If after two hours we didn't take them out of the cage, they wouldn't eat, they wouldn't drink," Lüscher said. "They'd die quickly, but very happily."

Humans may not like to think they have much in common with monkeys or rats. Addiction can occur when the normal process of a reward for positive behavior or experiences goes wrong. For example, people feel good when they eat a piece of cake because it tastes good and sugar is a concentrated form of nutrition and energy. Human ancestors seldom came across any sweet food with concentrated calories, much less slices of tasty birthday cake. Ancient human brains offered a big dopamine reward if they came across honey or sweet fruits which were rare, important calorie and nutrition boosts. The human dopamine reward system doesn't understand that today, cake or other sweets are available at almost any time. The dopamine reward system can lead to addiction to sweets or other foods that are best consumed rarely and in small quantities.

Fentanyl is so addictive because it causes such a strong release of dopamine when it binds to the mu opioid receptor in our brains. So much dopamine is released that it results in the **euphoria** and "high" feeling associated with fentanyl and other opiates.

The Brain Disease Model of Addiction

Because addiction causes people to behave in ways that are out of their direct control, people may assume that addicts have moral problems or are "weak" and unable to stop taking drugs or drinking alcohol. Physical changes occur in the brain of an addicted person which influence their ability to control their substance use. Addiction is a complex process which involves physical dependency and behavior oriented toward getting the addictive substance.

The brain disease model of addiction has emerged to help scientists understand how the brain contributes to addiction and develop ways to treat it. Some people are more vulnerable to developing addictions because of the composition of their brains, and different people's brains are vulnerable to different substances. Not everyone who takes fentanyl will become addicted to it, just as not everyone who drinks alcohol becomes an alcoholic.

In addition to the flood of dopamine which results from taking an addictive substance like fentanyl, human brains have specific dopamine receptors called D_2 receptors. These determine how motivated a person will be to work toward a long-term reward, or how much that person will prefer smaller, immediate rewards.

People with D_2 receptors that respond less to dopamine tend to be more impulsive than those with more responsive D_2 receptors. This is one of the brain characteristics that contributes to addictive behavior. The trait doesn't mean a person will become addicted to any substance, including fentanyl. It simply means they could be at greater risk.

Addictive substances add to the problem by reducing the capacity of D_2 receptors through continued substance use. This process leads to drug tolerance and dependency. Fentanyl is so powerful that it can quickly dampen D_2 receptors, leading to a need for more and more of the drug to produce the same feeling. The less responsive D_2 receptors are, the harder it is for a person who has become addicted to enter recovery.

How Does Fentanyl Kill?

"Taking fentanyl on the street is like playing Russian roulette," according to Dr. Lisa Bishop, interim dean of Memorial University's School of Pharmacy. Russian roulette is a deadly game played by putting a single bullet into a revolver and spinning the chambers, then pointing the gun at one's head and pulling the trigger.

To watch how fentanyl can kill, scan here:

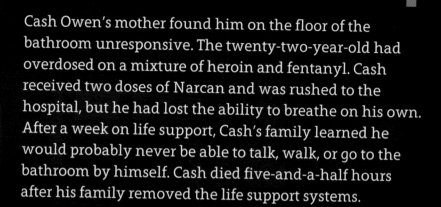

Cash Owen's mother found him on the floor of the bathroom unresponsive. The twenty-two-year-old had overdosed on a mixture of heroin and fentanyl. Cash received two doses of Narcan and was rushed to the hospital, but he had lost the ability to breathe on his own. After a week on life support, Cash's family learned he would probably never be able to talk, walk, or go to the bathroom by himself. Cash died five-and-a-half hours after his family removed the life support systems.

When someone takes fentanyl, the drug enters their blood. It enters instantly if injected and more slowly if taken through a patch, lollipop, or pill. Once fentanyl is in the blood, the substance quickly travels to the brain, spinal cord, and nerves, where it attaches to opioid receptors.

In the brain, fentanyl's molecules attach to parts of the brain that produce dopamine, the chemical which produces feelings of happiness and well-being. Fentanyl is so powerful that a massive amount of dopamine is quickly released.

Fentanyl also affects the part of our brain that controls normal sleep and breathing. The part of the brain that controls breathing is our respiratory center, located at the base of the brain. Under normal circumstances, our brain automatically responds to how much oxygen and carbon monoxide we have in the blood, directing how often we breathe. Fentanyl interferes with this process. It can slow breathing and potentially bring it to a stop. Although fentanyl

Photo illustration of 2 milligrams of fentanyl—a lethal dose for most people.

in proper doses is used as anesthesia for heart surgery, an overdose slows the heart as well as the lungs. Too much fentanyl interferes with the normal signals that keep a person breathing and his or her heart beating. This can lead to cardiac arrest: a heart attack.

Without enough oxygen, the brain and other organs begin to shut down. Other effects can include foaming at the mouth due to lung inflammation and vomiting because fentanyl can block the body's natural gag reflexes. People who overdose on fentanyl may vomit and then aspirate (breathe in) the vomit, which will also stop breathing by clogging their lungs.

A vial of naloxone, which can be used to reverse the effects of a heroin overdose.

With their brains starved of oxygen, people who overdose on fentanyl can have seizures. After four minutes without oxygen, permanent brain damage begins to occur. Some people who've been brought back from fentanyl overdoses with the antidote Narcan have suffered permanent effects, similar to a person who has had a stroke. They may become paralyzed or lose the ability to speak.

Naloxone can Reverse Fentanyl Overdoses

Fentanyl, morphine, and heroin are opioid **agonists**, which means they bind to opioid receptors and cause the release of dopamine and other brain chemicals. Drugs that cause the opposite effect on opioid receptors are called opioid antagonists. When the antagonist binds to the opioid receptor, it displaces the effect of the agonist drug.

Naloxone, also called Narcan, is an opioid antagonist that binds to the mu opioid receptor (MOP), bumping fentanyl off. Naloxone is injectable and can also be used as a nasal spray. It is very fast-acting and lasts for 30 to 90 minutes. Because fentanyl is fat-soluble and was designed to be very strong, it can reattach after a dose of naloxone and re-initiate overdose symptoms. Repeated large doses of naloxone may be required to reverse a fentanyl overdose. If an overdose has led to damage to the brain or other organs like the heart, lungs, and liver, Naloxone can't reverse those effects. Sometimes emergency responders arrive too late and Naloxone cannot reverse the overdose.

TEXT-DEPENDENT QUESTIONS

1. What are the four types of opioid receptors?
2. What is the Brain Disease model of addiction?
3. What is dopamine?

RESEARCH PROJECT

Read more about the behaviors that contribute to substance addiction. Compare and contrast an unhealthy and dangerous addiction like fentanyl or alcohol addiction with a healthy daily habit like exercise. What are the similarities and what are the differences? Write a one-page essay describing the elements of each that you compare and contrast. Include your sources at the end of the essay.

Fentanyl is so potentially dangerous that DEA agents wear protective clothing when gathering evidence inside of illegal drug-processing facilities. The drug is easily absorbed through contact with the skin, and a tiny amount could be potent enough to kill.

WORDS TO UNDERSTAND

adverse—a quality or characteristic that is harmful or unfavorable.

naive—innocent or unexposed. A person who has never taken a medication is "naive" to the effects of that medication.

side effects—undesirable and potentially dangerous effects of a medication.

tremors—trembling or shaking in body parts, especially the hands, which interferes with normal movement.

CHAPTER 4

THE LONG-TERM EFFECTS OF FENTANYL

Opioids mimic the body's natural pain and stress relieving hormones when they bind to receptors in neural cells, but unlike the chemicals our bodies make naturally, they are addictive and cause physical and cognitive **side effects**.

Some people use the terms "dependency" and "addiction" interchangeably, but they do not mean the same thing. Fentanyl, like any other opioid, produces dependency, which refers to the body's need or dependence on the drug for normal functioning. Physical symptoms result after a person stops taking the drug, often referred to as withdrawal.

Addiction refers to the continuing need to take a drug, both psychologically and physically. Not every person who takes fentanyl becomes addicted. Like other opioids, fentanyl has a high potential for addiction. Some people who have only taken fentanyl one time become addicted and feel an overwhelming desire to take it again and again.

What Is Opioid/Fentanyl Dependency?

The Centers for Disease Control sampled 10 percent of the medical records of more than 1.2 million people who were prescribed opioids between 2006 and 2015. Out of this group, even among patients who were only prescribed opioids for one day, 6 percent had a probability of continuing to take the drugs after one year. After three years, 2.9 percent had a probability of still taking opioids. The study discovered that dependency on opioids could occur in as little as five days.

Fentanyl patches are a long-acting opioid, which fits in the category that the CDC study found to be at the highest risk for addiction and dependency. Oxycodone (often sold under the brand name OxyContin) was the most-commonly prescribed and most-addictive opioid in this category. More than 27 percent of people who received a thirty-day supply of oxycodone were still using it one year later, and more than 20 percent were still using it three years later. People who use prescription opioids for a year or longer are considered "chronic" users.

Dependency on an opioid means that people don't just need to take the drug to relieve pain, they need to take it to function in general. Physicians sometimes refer to people who have never taken opioids before as "opioid **naive**." A person who is opioid naive will need a lower dose of the drug to get pain relief, while a person who is accustomed to taking the opioid will need a higher dose. Because of the way opioids, including fentanyl, work in the body, anyone who takes them over a long period of time will develop a tolerance. Tolerance for a medication means that higher and higher doses are needed to produce the desired effect. In the case of patients taking fentanyl for chronic, severe pain, they may lose the benefits of even ultra-strong fentanyl and no longer have relief of their pain.

Michael Wolman, a patient of the University Health Network in Toronto, Canada, had multiple painful conditions including scoliosis, arthritis, and fibromyalgia. Michael took several types of opioids for years, including Percocet, OxyContin, hydromorphone, and fentanyl. Michael's life consisted of waiting for the clock to show him it was time to take the next dose of medicine because he had become tolerant of all of the opioids, including fentanyl. "The medicine was no longer serving the pain," Michael said. "It was serving itself."

To learn more about fentanyl dependence, scan here:

In 2018, singer Demi Lovato nearly died after overdosing on oxycodone that had been laced with fentanyl.

Higher doses of any opioid, including fentanyl, have a higher chance of producing negative side effects associated with opioids. Physicians call undesirable side effects **adverse** drug reactions. The most serious adverse drug reaction for fentanyl and other opioids is an overdose. Less-serious side effects include nausea, vomiting, constipation, sedation, and itchy skin. More serious side effects can include low blood pressure, depressed breathing, and hallucinations.

If someone has developed a dependency on fentanyl and needs the drug for physical reasons, they will suffer withdrawal symptoms once they stop taking it. Withdrawal symptoms can be severe and potentially fatal, depending on how much fentanyl the person was taking and how long they have been taking it.

Side Effects and Risks

Side effects of fentanyl vary depending on how it is taken. People who use fentanyl patches for pain may experience skin reactions on the site where they use the patch, including blisters, sores, rashes, and swelling of the skin. The medication can cause dizziness or light-headedness and drowsiness. People who use fentanyl patches shouldn't drive until or unless they've checked with their doctor and know they will be alert enough to operate a car. They may feel nauseated or even vomit, especially when they are first using the patch.

Fentanyl shares one of the most common side effects of opioids: constipation. These drugs slow the nervous system, which slows down the process of digestion. Over time, a condition called opioid-induced bowel dysfunction (OIBD) can develop. This condition isn't just inconvenient, it can reduce someone's ability to move and go about daily life. Because people who take opioids for pain often have reduced mobility, the condition is difficult to treat and there are few options to relieve it.

Fentanyl has powerful effects on the central nervous system, including the brain. Cognitive side effects of long-term use can include anxiety, confusion, and **tremors** similar to Parkinson's disease.

Parkinson's disease is a central nervous system (CNS) disorder caused by nerve cell damage in the brain that leads to less dopamine, the important neurotransmitting hormone. In and of itself, Parkinson's disease is not fatal, but

Opioids like fentanyl make it harder for the user to focus. They also reduce the user's coordination and reaction time, and can cause blurred vision. These side effects can have a serious effect on the user's driving ability, leading to accidents.

its effects on the body reduce quality of life and lead to other life-threatening conditions like pneumonia and blood clots. Fentanyl use can cause the symptoms of Parkinson's disease by interfering with the body's normal production of dopamine leading to tremors, slowed movement, and speech and writing changes.

The primary risk of fentanyl is overdose. The drug is so powerful that patients using prescribed fentanyl could overdose easily. People taking fentanyl from street dealers run the risk of overdosing any time they take any substance with fentanyl in it, whether it is heroin or cocaine cut with fentanyl, or pills made from fentanyl mixed with powdered milk or glucose that they have been told are weaker opioids like Vicodin.

Symptoms of fentanyl overdose are severe drowsiness or the inability to wake or be awakened, pinpoint pupils in the eyes, seizures, slow heartbeat, and very slow, difficult breathing.

Risks of Fentanyl Patches

People using fentanyl patches have to be cautious. The patch is designed to slowly release fentanyl over two to three days. If a patient accidentally touches the gel or gets it into their mouth, they will receive a much stronger dose and could overdose.

Fentanyl patches must be kept out of the reach of children or pets. More than thirty young children have overdosed, some fatally, from finding fentanyl patches and putting them in their mouths or sticking them on their bodies. A toddler boy accidentally got a fentanyl patch on one of his toys while playing at his grandmother's nursing home. Returning home, the boy's mother thought there was a band-aid on his toy truck, but it turned out to be a carelessly discarded fentanyl

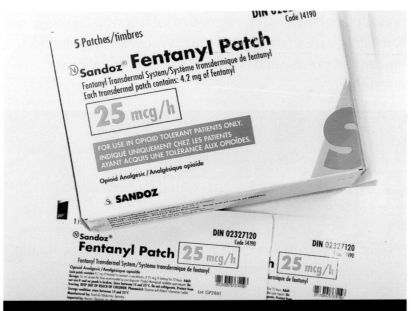

Transdermal fentanyl patches can be very dangerous to young children or pets, because contact with them quickly delivers the drug into the bloodstream.

patch. While playing, the boy put the patch in his mouth. He died within a short time.

Fentanyl lollipops (Actiq) are as potentially deadly as patches, but have been found responsible for fewer accidental poisonings than patches.

Pets are also at risk. Dogs have licked or chewed fentanyl patches they found in the trash, and died. The FDA advises patients to throw their used patches away by folding them with the sticky sides together and flushing them down the toilet. The patch's ability to provide pain relief may be gone in after three days, but 50 percent of the fentanyl in the gel is still active—more than enough to seriously hurt or kill a small child or animal.

The Drug Enforcement Administration (DEA) hosts national drug take-back days and local health agencies may also accept prescription medications for safe disposal. All unused prescription drugs may be turned in for disposal this way, but some drugs are so dangerous the FDA advises they should immediately be flushed down the toilet when no longer needed.

DANGEROUS DRUGS

The FDA maintains a list of thirteen medicines that people should flush down the toilet immediately when they no longer need them, because they are too dangerous to leave around the house. Fentanyl, OxyContin, Demerol, and Vicodin are some of the common opioids on the "must flush" list.

Opioid Tolerance

Fentanyl is such a powerful drug that when physicians prescribe it for pain, they only do so with "opioid tolerant" patients. Opioid tolerance means that a person can tolerate a higher dose of an opioid medication than others. An opioid tolerant patient has a less-than-expected response to receiving opioid medication. Diagnosis and prescription becomes complex because people can be naturally opioid-tolerant and need higher doses to receive pain relief. Most opioid tolerance, however, is acquired. Physicians are cautious about the amount of opioids they prescribe for "opioid naive" patients: people who have never taken any kind of opioid medication.

Fentanyl is never prescribed for opioid naive patients. Fentanyl is officially labeled for use only with patients who have taken at least 60 milligrams of oral morphine a day and aren't getting enough pain relief. They must be taking at least 150 milligrams of codeine, or 30 milligrams of oxycodone, to qualify for fentanyl.

People who haven't taken any of these drugs or street heroin are always opioid naive and could risk overdose and even death taking any amount of fentanyl at all. The FDA advises people who have even touched a small portion of the gel on a fentanyl patch to wash thoroughly with water, not use soap, and seek immediate medical treatment.

The Mental Side Effects

Some studies of small numbers of patients receiving fentanyl for chronic cancer pain have shown that after a few months of use, the patients didn't show decreases in memory, language, attention abilities, or ability to drive. The patients in these studies were receiving medically monitored, limited doses of fentanyl in patch form. Some patients even showed improvement on cognitive tests. Pain affects mental and physical abilities, and several studies indicate that the pain relief provided by patches outweighed any negative effects of fentanyl on their cognitive abilities.

Tests of illicit opioids and their effect on thinking and reaction time show slowed reaction times, mental clouding, confusion, and lack of energy. Treatment centers serving people who've become addicted to fentanyl say that in addition to the physical effects of dependency and mental effects of addiction itself, addicts show poor judgment in relationships, at work, or in school or social situations. Fentanyl, like other opioids, causes long-term changes and damage to many different parts of the brain. Fentanyl

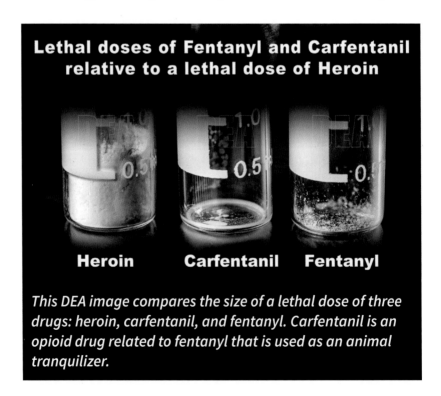

Lethal doses of Fentanyl and Carfentanil relative to a lethal dose of Heroin

Heroin   **Carfentanil**   **Fentanyl**

This DEA image compares the size of a lethal dose of three drugs: heroin, carfentanil, and fentanyl. Carfentanil is an opioid drug related to fentanyl that is used as an animal tranquilizer.

also makes any pre-existing or co-occurring mental health problems worse.

Heroin has been known as an addictive opioid much longer than fentanyl and more studies have been conducted on how it damages the brain and nervous system. MRI imaging of long-term heroin addicts shows observable changes in their brains, including less brain tissue, particularly gray matter. Heroin addicts experience changed and damaged tissue in areas that control vision and hearing, emotions, speech, and memory. In losing healthy brain tissue, addicts experience a loss of emotional and impulse control. Severe long-term addicts even lose the ability to make simple decisions or the ability to understand when and how to eat properly.

How Mental and Physical Health Contribute to Fentanyl Addiction

Some people turn to using illegal drugs because they have an underlying mental or physical health diagnosis and they are seeking relief. Addiction and recovery professionals call this tendency "self-medicating." A co-occurring disorder simply means that a person who is addicted to a substance like fentanyl also has a physical or mental illness that affects their ability to recover and that is almost certain to be worsened by drug misuse.

Researchers already know that taking opioids can lead to long-term addiction after only five days. A 2014 Clemson University study discovered that student-athletes are more vulnerable than others to misusing prescription painkillers and that football players were the most-vulnerable to misuse opioids. The study of 2,300 high school athletes found that 12 percent of male athletes and 8 percent of female athletes had misused prescription painkilling drugs in the previous year.

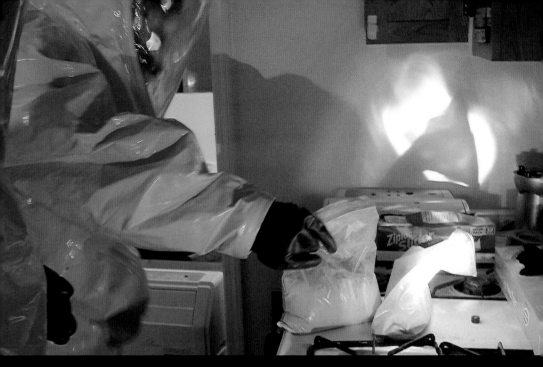

A federal agent investigates a suspected drug laboratory where fentanyl is being processed.

Sports injuries and recurring pain are one type of co-occurring disorder. "Young people also may look to stronger drugs for euphoric effects," said Bryan Denham, the author of the Clemson study.

Other underlying co-occurring disorders that can contribute to fentanyl or other opioid addiction and be worsened by it include depression, anxiety disorders, or post-traumatic stress disorder (PTSD). Opioids, including fentanyl, cause an artificial, chemically induced rush of euphoria and good feelings that can provide temporary relief from the sadness of depression or fears of anxiety. Over time, fentanyl destroys the natural ability to create dopamine or react to natural endorphins. An already-depressed person isn't making themselves better by taking an opioid like fentanyl. They are making it difficult, and in some cases almost impossible, to improve their mental health without help.

TEXT-DEPENDENT QUESTIONS

1. What does it mean to be opioid naive? To be opioid tolerant?
2. What are some of the long-term effects of fentanyl abuse on the brain and central nervous system?
3. Compare and contrast the differences between dependency and addiction to fentanyl, using information from the chapter.

RESEARCH PROJECT

The FDA recommends that people flush dangerous medicines like fentanyl down the toilet if they are no longer being used and people don't have access to an official disposal site. Using the internet, read more about how medicines can get into rivers and streams and why the FDA advises this method of disposal for fentanyl and other dangerous drugs. Write a one page report about whether or not you agree with the FDA's instructions or think that dangerous medicines could still cause harm if they get into the water supply. Include your sources.

Group therapy sessions, in which addicts share their experiences, are often a component of drug treatment programs.

 WORDS TO UNDERSTAND

craving—a strong and potentially uncontrollable need for a substance, whether drugs or food.

precipitating—a start or initial occurrence that leads to later events.

substance use disorder (SUD)—the healthcare term for addiction, including fentanyl addiction.

CHAPTER 5

TREATING FENTANYL ADDICTION

Addiction is a disease with physical and mental components. Fentanyl is so strong that anyone who becomes addicted to it will have a high opioid tolerance and will experience severe withdrawal symptoms when they stop taking it.

Another danger of fentanyl addiction comes after recovery. If someone successfully stops taking fentanyl and enters recovery, if they take fentanyl again, they are at an even higher risk of fatal overdose than they would have been before they recovered.

Treatment for fentanyl addiction is similar to treatment for addiction to other opioids. Medication may be used to help reduce withdrawal symptoms and provide time for people to recover physically and mentally from fentanyl misuse during early recovery. Later phases of recovery can differ. Everyone who becomes addicted to any substance including fentanyl needs to maintain recovery through good mental and physical health habits and is at-risk of potential relapse.

Entering Treatment

Like other opioids, fentanyl has powerful physical and mental effects that result in withdrawal symptoms once someone stops taking it. Addicts can have moderate withdrawal symptoms including a loss of appetite, fever and chills, a runny nose or cough, and nausea and vomiting. More serious withdrawal symptoms can include tremors and even seizures.

To prevent deaths due to fentanyl and other opioids, New York's Department of Health and Mental Hygiene holds "overdose reversal" classes, in which people are trained to administer naloxone in emergency situations.

Fentanyl: The World's Deadliest Drug

Cognitive symptoms of withdrawal can include agitation, anxiety and panic, and intense **cravings** for the drug.

Many people who are addicted to fentanyl are also addicted to other substances, including heroin, marijuana, cocaine, and alcohol. This type of addiction is called polydrug addiction. A fentanyl addict can choose to enter treatment because of an event that shocks them into realizing they need help. This is called a **precipitating** event. With fentanyl use disorders, it could be an overdose or near-death experience or witnessing a friend dying from an overdose.

Most people who stop taking fentanyl undergo a period of medically supervised detoxification or "detox." The goal of detox is simply to remove fentanyl and its effects from the body so that the addict can begin to make better conscious health choices and enter rehabilitation programs.

Detox can be painful, humiliating, and mentally and physically exhausting. The Truth Initiative produced an anti-opioid PSA showing the first three days of detox for Rebekkah (known by her first name only), a twenty-six-year old woman who first became addicted to opioids after injuring her ankle at age fourteen during cheerleading practice.

The Truth Initiative showed Rebekkah's detox for three days via a video kiosk on the streets in New York City. Onlookers gathered throughout the day and a shortened YouTube version has over 100,000 views. After suffering nausea, vomiting and severe drug cravings, by the third day, Rebekkah said, "I have a lot of self-image issues. My mind doesn't tell me anything nice. When I look in the mirror I see nothing."

Her sober living coach said that this feeling of disconnection or "being nothing" was a symptom of depression and also right where Rebekkah needed to be: a normal part of the detox process.

Scan here to see excerpts from Rebekkah's opioid detox:

What Is an Intervention?

An intervention is an organized event in which family, friends, and professionals confront an addicted person and convince them to willingly undergo treatment. The majority of interventions succeed on the day of the intervention, according to Family First Intervention, a professional drug and alcohol intervention organization. Intervention success rates increase if families follow through with professional guidelines and assistance. Unfortunately, only 10 percent of families that contact Families First go through with the intervention and complete the necessary steps that follow.

You may have seen episodes of *Intervention*, a show that began on the A&E Network in 2005. The show features professional, trained interventionists and family members who try to convince an addicted loved one to enter treatment. In the first 276 episodes of *Intervention*, 270 subjects had agreed to go into treatment. This is a 98.7 percent success rate at getting the addicts to recognize they had a problem and needed help. Of the 270 people who went into treatment, 151 (55 percent) remained clean and sober after several years.

This is a very high success rate. Alcoholics Anonymous (AA) and Narcotics Anonymous (NA) report long-term success rates of between 5 percent and 10 percent. One of the reasons *Intervention* is so much more successful than non-televised interventions is probably the show's process for choosing subjects. The show's staff receives between 300 and 900 applications for every show, and their main criteria for selecting subjects is the willingness to examine their own weaknesses and problems. "We strive to pick subjects that will be as brutally honest with us as we are direct with our questions," show-runner Jeff Weaver told *Business Insider* in 2015.

Overall, however, interventions are most likely to succeed if there is family involvement, as well as professional guidance and structure. Family First Intervention explains, "Intervention is for the family, while treatment is for the addict."

Recovery Programs

According to Family First Intervention, addiction is the only long-term, fatal illness that is 100 percent treatable. The organization also says that 90 percent of addicts believe that addiction is their fault. Research now shows that this is untrue. Addiction is a complex disorder and especially with an ultra-powerful drug like fentanyl, the drug itself causes effects that create addiction. Fentanyl was invented to help surgeons perform open heart surgery and as pain relief for the most extreme types of chronic pain, such as terminal cancer pain. It was never meant to be taken without a physician's supervision or as a recreational drug.

People addicted to fentanyl should undergo detox before entering any type of rehab program. While their bodies still contain fentanyl, it's impossible for them to participate successfully in counseling or rehab sessions.

Detox treats withdrawal symptoms and helps people who are addicted to fentanyl to overcome physical dependency. Further treatment can take several forms, from long-term residential treatment lasting longer than three months to short-term, 4-week residential treatment and intensive outpatient programs as a follow-up.

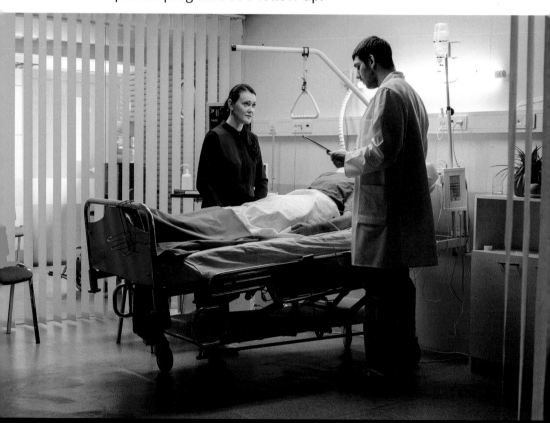

Because of the withdrawal symptoms that accompany dependence on opioids like fentanyl, addicts might need to rid their bodies of the drug in a hospital setting.

Most addiction specialists believe that recovering from opioid dependency, including fentanyl, takes at least a year. During this time, whether they are living in a drug- and alcohol-free rehab facility or at home, addicts may receive medication-assisted treatment (MAT). Medication-assisted treatment was first developed for heroin addiction in the 1970s. Methadone, an opioid that doesn't cause a euphoric "high" was distributed to addicts via methadone clinics. Instead of being injected, methadone was provided in liquid form. Early methadone programs just provided the alternate medication without counseling or other support.

Today, medication-assisted treatment (MAT) for opioid addiction, including fentanyl, may include other medications in addition to methadone, including buprenorphine and naltrexone. These medications don't offer a euphoric "drug high" but do help to heal the neurotransmitting pathways in the nervous system that fentanyl, heroin, or other opioid abuse has disrupted.

Medication-assisted treatment (MAT) is always combined with group or individual therapy. A fentanyl addict may start out in a three-month residential treatment program where they will eat a nutritious diet, practice mindfulness techniques like yoga and meditation, and participate in group and individual therapy. Twelve-step programs based on Alcoholics Anonymous (AA) and Narcotics Anonymous (NA) are also a part of many residential rehab programs. Twelve-step programs are also referred to as "self-help" or community-based programs.

After completing residential treatment, fentanyl addicts may return home and participate in an intensive outpatient program (IOP) or regular outpatient program. IOPs are sometimes also called partial hospitalization programs (PHP) if they last longer than three hours a day. An intensive

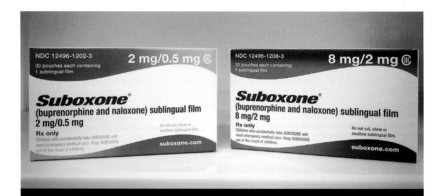

Suboxone, a prescription medication that includes both buprenorphine and naloxone, is sometimes prescribed to help mitigate the physical cravings of those addicted to opiates. These drugs interact with the opiate receptors in the brain, but do not provide the same "high" as fentanyl.

outpatient program (IOP) lasts at least three hours per session, three times per week. Regular outpatient programs meet at least once a week, and sessions last less than three hours.

Longer-term programs can include sober living homes, which are an outgrowth of "halfway houses" that emerged during the 1970s. Sober living homes provide a safe living environment free of drugs and alcohol for addicts who have completed residential treatment. People who live in sober living homes usually have to work at least part-time, and are expected to pay to live in the home and attend meetings like AA or NA.

Both residential treatment and outpatient treatment programs can be effective. The difference isn't the environment so much as it is the length of time an addictive person participates. According to the National Institute on Drug Abuse (NIDA), whether an addict participates in residential or outpatient treatment, a program needs to last 90 days or longer for a lasting outcome. NIDA's research has discovered that methadone or other medication-assisted treatment (MAT) should be continued for at least a year for lasting results. Dropping out of treatment is the major cause of relapse. Addicts can't "do it on their own" and if they attend a treatment program for a short time and then quit believing they can "help themselves," they are almost certain to relapse. Some treatment programs combine a four-week stay in a residential rehab facility with two to three months of intensive outpatient treatment (IOP). People who are receiving medication-assisted treatment (MAT) for fentanyl addiction should count on taking the medication for at least a year and attending group and individual therapy and outpatient treatment meetings. Most programs also encourage attendance at self-help twelve-step meetings in addition to formal treatment.

What Is a Dual Diagnosis and How Does it Affect Fentanyl Recovery?

Dual diagnosis is also referred to as a co-occurring disorder. The term is used by healthcare professionals to refer to someone experiencing a mental illness and a **substance use disorder** at the same time. Either condition could have developed first. Some people with mental illness turn to drugs and/or alcohol to relieve their mental health symptoms. Others develop mental illness as a result of their substance use.

Fentanyl and other opiates can easily cause depression with overuse, because they disrupt the brain's normal ability to cope with stress, pain, or feel pleasure. If the only pleasure or happiness a person feels comes from a strong opioid like fentanyl, once the substance is removed, they are likely to feel depressed.

As many as 90 percent of fentanyl addicts started out taking milder opioids like OxyContin or Vicodin. They may

Rapper Mac Miller died in September 2018 from an accidental overdose of fentanyl, cocaine, and alcohol. He had been suffering from clinical depression for years, and used the drugs in a desperate attempt to alleviate the symptoms of his mental illness.

have been prescribed these medications for a sports injury like Rebekkah, who injured her ankle during cheerleading practice. Others may receive opioids for chronic back pain. Injuries and illnesses like cancer or Ehlers-Danlos Syndrome, a chronic inherited disease which affects joints, skin, and blood vessels leading to severe pain, are other forms of co-occurring disorders. The term "dual diagnosis" is usually used to refer to mental illness that is diagnosed along with a substance use disorder. According to the National Alliance for the Mentally Ill (NAMI) 7.9 million people in the US have a mental illness and a substance use disorder.

Successful treatment for fentanyl addicts with co-occurring mental or physical illnesses will address the mental illness and/or physical illness which is occurring at the same time as the addiction. Some additions to treatment that people with dual diagnosis benefit from include supportive housing, which provides a place to live and support for drug-free, healthier daily living, and psychotherapy, especially cognitive behavioral therapy (CBT) which helps people to develop coping skills and healthier patterns of thinking.

Prospects for Recovery

The odds for long-term recovery for people who are addicted to any substance are in and of themselves, sobering. Even if a person has stopped using an addictive substance, they are never truly "cured." They are in recovery as long as they aren't using the substance. In the case of fentanyl, returning to using it can be fatal very quickly. Once a person has been in recovery for several months and has stopped using fentanyl, even the tiniest amount of the ultra-strong opioid could cause an overdose.

Addiction is a chronic disease like high blood pressure (hypertension), diabetes, and asthma. Relapse rates for these diseases and addiction are similar. Fifty to 70 percent of people with hypertension relapse within one year of receiving treatment while 40 to 60 percent of people with addiction relapse within a year, according to the National Institute on Drug Abuse (NIDA). These statistics are the reason why "harm reduction" programs have been introduced. A "harm reduction" program seeks to reduce the amount of harm an addicted person can do to their own health and to others, including family, friends, and the community.

In the case of fentanyl, the drug is so powerful and the risks of overdose so great, it is hard to imagine how a person using fentanyl could "use less" as part of a harm-reduction program. Medication-assisted treatment (MAT) can be seen as part of harm-reduction because the medications used are opioids. They just do not produce a euphoric "high" or encourage criminal activity like heroin or fentanyl.

According to the Substance Abuse and Mental Health Services Administration (SAMHSA), 11.5 million people ages twelve and older misused prescription pain relievers in 2016. Of this group, 228,000 misused fentanyl. That year, 23,000 people died from fentanyl overdoses—about 10 percent of those who misused fentanyl. With such a high rate of death, fentanyl recovery rates aren't like the recovery rates for the commonly abused prescription opioids, like oxycodone. One out of ten people who misuse fentanyl can never recover, because they are dead.

Because fentanyl often appears in the form of a fine powder, it is easy to mix into other drugs like heroin or cocaine to increase their potency.